Animal Talents

By Clem King

Contents

Some animals have a talent for hunting.

Other animals are great at staying silent and hiding.

Some animals even use their talents to help each other.

Hunting Talents

Spiders spin sticky webs to catch insects. They can make their webs between some branches.

Some spiders use venom to kill the insects that get stuck in the web.

Tigers have a talent for hiding. Their stripes help them blend into the background.

From its hiding spot, the silent tiger hunts its prey.

In just a few seconds, the tiger can pounce!

Komodo dragons are big reptiles that can run fast.

They can also use their claws to chase their prey up trees.

Other Talents

An octopus has a great method for hiding.
It changes the colour of its skin to match the rock.

Can you see an octopus?

A camel can walk for days before it needs a drink.
It can keep water in its blood.

What a crazy talent!

Seals have thick blubber to keep out the cold.

They can swim in very cold water and even lie on frozen land.

A Talent for Teamwork

Some animals use their talents as a team.

Egrets treat this buffalo like a hotel!
They can stay safe up on the buffalo's back.

The egrets help the buffalo by pecking off bugs that bite the buffalo's skin.

Zebras and ostriches have a method for protecting each other from big cats.

Ostriches can see a long way away, and zebras can smell the big cats.

They try not to panic, and they alert each other!

Animals all over our planet have talents to help them hunt, stay safe and be happy.

CHECKING FOR MEANING

1. Where is one place that spiders make their webs? *(Literal)*
2. What talents do zebras and ostriches have to protect each other from big cats? *(Literal)*
3. Why do you think the egrets peck the bugs off the buffalo's skin? *(Inferential)*
4. Which animal do you think gets the best result from working together: the buffalo or the egrets? *(Evaluative)*

EXTEND VOCABULARY

silent	What is another word with a similar meaning to *silent*? What is the opposite of *silent*?
venom	What other animals have venom? What other word do you know that has a similar meaning to *venom*?
blubber	Do you know any other animals that have blubber to keep their bodies warm?

MOVING BEYOND THE TEXT

1. The animals in this text have many different skills. What skill or talent would you like to have?
2. What other skills or talents do animals have?
3. Choose one animal from the text. What else do you know about that animal?
4. Do you have any special skills? What do your talents help you do?

TIME TO WRITE

Write a story about an octopus that uses its talent for hiding. Why does it need to hide? Where does it hide?